THROUGH THE SEASONS

Pond

Deni Bown

Illustrated by Wendy Meadway

Through the Seasons

Field and Hedgerow
Garden
Park
Pond
Stream
Wood

Edited by Marcella Streets
Designed by Charles Harford HSD

First published in 1989 by
Wayland (Publishers) Ltd
61 Western Road, Hove
East Sussex BN3 1JD, England

British Cataloguing in Publication Data
Bown, Deni
   Pond.—(Through the Seasons).
   1. Great Britain. Organisms. Habitats
   I. Title II. Meadway, Wendy III. Series
   574.5'2

ISBN 1 85210 753 7

Phototypeset by DP Press, Sevenoaks, Kent
Printed in Italy by G. Canale & C.S.p.A., Turin
Bound in Belgium by Casterman S.A.

CONTENTS

Words that appear in **bold** in the text
are explained in the glossary on page 30.

WHAT IS A POND?

A pond is a large pool of still water.

Ponds form in hollows of land which have little or no drainage. They are smaller than lakes and not as deep. Most ponds in mountains and woodland are natural, but those in villages, farms and gardens have usually been made by people. Water seeps into ponds from surrounding land when it rains or snows. At the same time, water is lost when it **evaporates** from the pond's surface. It is also lost as animals drink it and plants use it for growth. In very hot, dry weather, some ponds almost dry up, but most have water all year.

4

Some villages still have ponds, but many have been filled in.

In the past, almost every country family kept a few animals for food and transport. There were no water pipes and taps, so ponds were dug for the animals to drink from. When horse-drawn vehicles were replaced by motor transport and modern water supplies became available, ponds were no longer needed. Many became overgrown or **polluted**.

◀ Many different plants and animals live in lowland ponds.

Ponds in woods, gravel pits and old quarries are usually surrounded by waterside plants and young willow or alder trees. They contain many insects, **amphibians** and other **aquatic** animals. Upland ponds in mountain and moorland areas have fewer plants and animals.

◀ **Green slime on ponds is a mass of plants called algae.**

Any pool of water, however small, attracts living things. If you leave a bowl of water outside, it soon turns green and slimy. **Algae** give out bubbles of **oxygen**, a gas needed by all living things. They grow from **spores** which are already present in the water or are carried there by the wind.

Ponds contain many tiny creatures, such as water fleas.

The food chain

When a pond forms, the algae are soon joined by other living things. Water fleas reach the water as minute eggs on birds' feet or in the mud on water plants. They feed on algae and swim by making jerky movements with their feelers. Algae and water fleas are eaten by animals such as snails, insects and fish, so these may be attracted to the pond as well. In turn, these creatures attract amphibians, birds and aquatic **mammals** such as water voles.

Plants make their own food using air, sunshine and water, but animals have to eat plants or other animals. Each living thing eats another, and that in turn eats something else. This is called a **food chain**. For example, a heron eats a fish which has eaten a snail that lives on pond weed. The lives of all the animals in a **community** depend on each other and they all depend on the plants.

◀ **Alder trees have catkin flowers in the spring**.

Alder trees grow in wet places. They have two kinds of flowers: male and female. The male flowers release **pollen** from dangling catkins on to purplish egg-shaped female flowers. Seeds then start to grow inside cone-like fruits. When ripe, the fruits turn woody and dark brown, opening so that the seeds fall out.

The silky flower buds of the willow tree are called pussy willow.

Willow trees are often found beside ponds. They produce catkin flowers in the spring before the new leaves appear. These are protected by soft silvery hairs. The male flowers produce bright yellow pollen.

▶

Marsh marigolds have bright yellow flowers.

The marsh marigold grows in wet mud and shallow water at the edge of ponds. Bees, flies and beetles visit its flowers to feed on **nectar** which is hidden in the centre. As they move about on each flower, their bodies pick up pollen from the male parts of the flower and brush it against the female parts. This is called **pollination**. As soon as this happens, the seeds inside the female part begin to develop.

◀ In late spring the bogbean produces spikes of white flowers.

The water in upland ponds is usually acidic because it seeps through **peat**. Bogbeans can grow in this acidic water. They often spread right across a pond with their creeping underwater stems. Their flowers attract bees and butterflies.

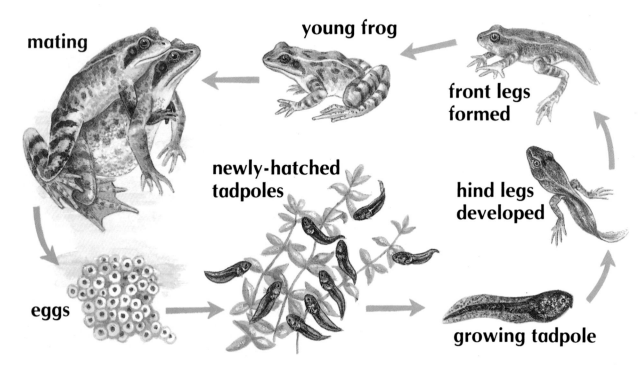

mating

young frog

front legs
formed

hind legs
developed

newly-hatched
tadpoles

growing tadpole

eggs

The life cycle of a frog

On the first warm days of spring,
frogs come out of **hibernation**.
The first thing they do is **mate**
and lay masses of eggs in the
water. After about a week, the
black dots begin to look more
like tadpoles. About ten days
later, the tadpoles are large
enough to wriggle out of the
jelly. At first, they eat algae. As
they get bigger, they feed on
water fleas and other small
animals. When they are seven
weeks old they start to grow
back legs. By the time they are

twelve weeks old, they have
front legs too. Then the tail
shrinks and the tiny froglets start
to hop about on land in search
of worms and insects.

Like frogs, newts are
amphibians and their **larvae** are
completely aquatic. Unlike
frogs, the female newt lays very
few eggs. She hides them one at
a time in the leaves of water
plants. Newt tadpoles grow
slowly and are **carnivorous**.
They do not lose their tails when
they turn into adults.

Toads spend more time on land than frogs. ▶

Toads are often found a long way from water, but every spring they return to **breed** at the pond where they hatched. During the breeding season, some ponds contain hundreds of toads, mating and laying eggs. Toadspawn is laid in long strings among underwater pond plants. You can tell a toad from a frog by its warty skin and because it walks rather than leaps.

Newts live on land but return to water to lay eggs.

◀ The moorhen nods its head and jerks its tail as it swims.

The moorhen has nothing to do with moors. Its name comes from 'mere', which is an old word for a lake. Moorhens have a croaking call. They like to eat fruit, seeds and water plants. They can sometimes be seen tiptoeing across water lily leaves, looking for insects.

Most pond snails eat algae and rotting plants. ▶

A number of different snails are found in ponds. The picture shows a giant pond snail. Snail eggs, in their blobs of jelly, can be found on underwater stones and on leaves. Snails and their eggs are eaten by fish and birds. Like land snails, pond snails move around on a band of slime. They can even glide along upside down under the surface of the water, hanging on by their slime trail.

THINGS TO DO IN SPRING

If you do not have a pond in your garden or at school, you can make a very small one for yourself. You will need an old sink or fish tank, or some other large container that measures about 60 cm long and at least 40 cm deep and wide. Stand it somewhere fairly shady, as the water will get too warm if it stands in the sun all day.

Put a layer of soil on the bottom of the container, followed by a layer of sand or gravel. Buy some aquatic plants from a garden centre or ask someone with a pond to give you a few. Plant them in pots of soil and stand them on the bottom of your pond, weighing them down with small stones. Then put a large stone in your pond and fill it up with water. Aim the water at the stone so that the mud is not stirred up. Most pond plants grow very quickly. They need trimming regularly so that they do not take over the whole pond.

The pond will need to settle for a week before anything else can be added. Think carefully about what you put in your pond. Fish are lovely to watch, but they will eat most smaller animals. A few snails from an aquatic centre or a very small amount of frogspawn might be more suitable. Or you may decide to add nothing and wait to see what turns up!

The black dots in frogspawn will grow into tadpoles.

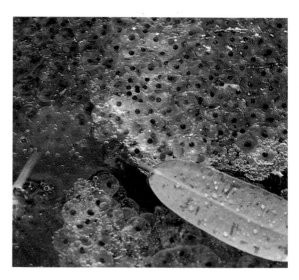

SUMMER

Water lilies have floating leaves and scented flowers.

Some pond plants, such as yellow irises and bur reeds, can grow in mud, but water lilies must have water at least 15 cm deep. Their leaves are known as lily pads. They are almost circular and usually lie flat on the water. Small birds, such as moorhens, and amphibians sometimes use them as stepping stones across the pond as they hunt for food.

Bur reed flowers are small and green.

You have to look carefully to find bur reed flowers. The male and female flowers are different. Both are ball-shaped but the male flower heads are smaller and higher up the stem. Bur reeds are pollinated by the wind, so they do not need colourful flowers to attract insects. The wind blows pollen from the male flowers to the female flowers, which then begin to develop seeds.

Tall yellow irises grow at the edge of the pond.

The large flowers of the yellow iris look lovely in early summer. Iris plants are often found in the wet mud beside ponds. They have flat, sword-shaped leaves and grow from thick, creeping, underground stems, which knit together in the soft mud.

Whirligig beetles move in circles on the pond surface.

▶

There are insects at every level of the pond: crawling in the mud at the bottom, swimming in the water, skimming on the surface and flying in the air above. Many insects lay their eggs in or near the water and their larvae develop under the surface.

Strange and interesting insects live in and around ponds.

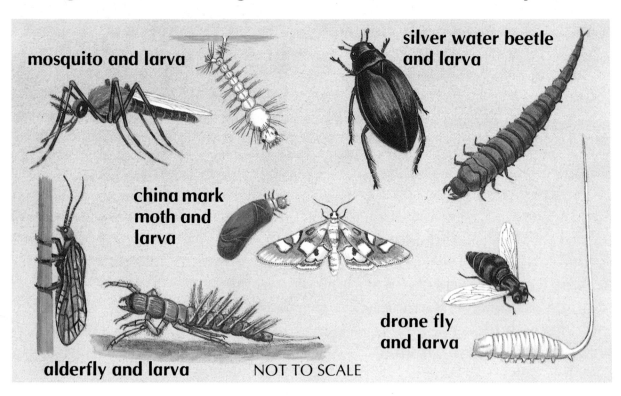

mosquito and larva

silver water beetle and larva

china mark moth and larva

drone fly and larva

alderfly and larva   NOT TO SCALE

16

◀ The great diving beetle is the fiercest insect in the water.

Adult great diving beetles are 3 to 4 cm long. They **prey** on any small pond creatures, including newts and fish that are bigger than they are. They breathe at the surface, trapping air under their wings, then dive using their strong, hairy back legs like oars. Their larvae are 6 cm long and eat about twenty tadpoles a day each!

The male stickleback builds a nest and protects the eggs. ▶

Sticklebacks are only about 10 cm long. In early summer the male's belly turns red to attract a mate. He makes a nest from pieces of pond plants and performs a zigzag dance for the female. The female lays 100 or more eggs in the nest. The male guards them for three weeks until they hatch.

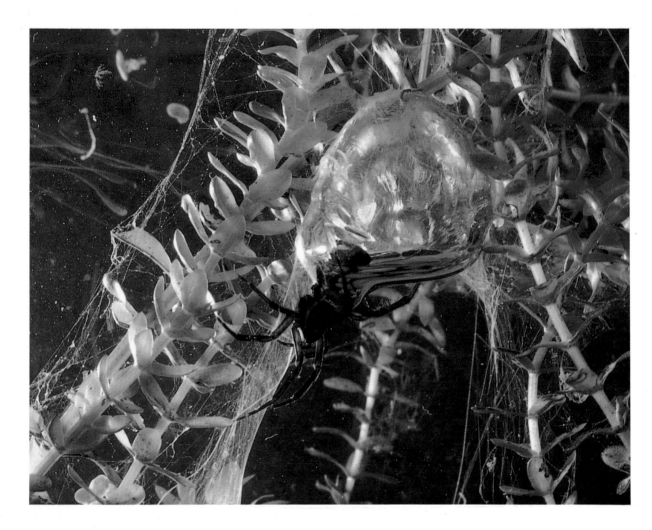

Water spiders live underwater in bubbles of air.

Only one kind of spider has discovered how to live completely underwater. The water spider makes a bell-shaped web. It fills it with air which it collects among its body hairs when it goes up to the surface. It lives in the bubble, darting out occasionally to catch water fleas or insect larvae. The female spider lays up to 100 eggs in the top of her bubble and the tiny spiders begin their lives underwater.

◄ Dragonflies dart at high speed over ponds.

Most dragonflies have brightly coloured bodies, very large eyes and two pairs of transparent wings. They are fast and powerful fliers. They twist and turn in the air, hovering and even flying backwards to catch their prey.

The life cycle of a dragonfly

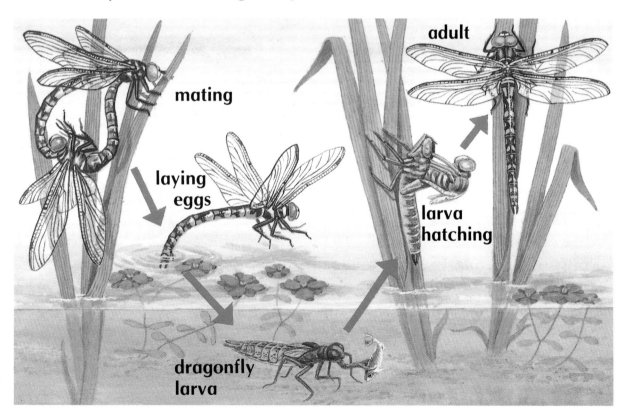

mating

laying eggs

adult

larva hatching

dragonfly larva

Carp are large, slow-moving fish which live a long time.

Wild carp are grey-brown in colour, but in aquatic centres you may see Japanese koi carp which are yellow, orange and white. If well cared for, carp can live for fifty years, reaching 120 cm long and over 25 kg in weight. Carp prefer deep ponds with muddy or sandy bottoms and plenty of water plants. They feed on plants and insect larvae. The female lays many thousands of eggs in the summer which hatch in a few days. Hardly any of the tiny fish survive. Most are eaten by other creatures.

Water voles may be seen nibbling at reeds beside the pond.

Although water voles are shy, they are active in the day so there is a good chance of seeing one, or at least of hearing a sudden 'plop' as it dives into the water. Water voles eat leaves, roots and nuts. They live in burrows and measure almost 20 cm in length, not counting the tail which is 10 cm long.

◄ The little water shrew kills fish and frogs with its poisonous bite.

Water shrews are less than half the size of water voles. Their long sensitive noses help them to find their prey. They are fast, skilful swimmers, darting around on the surface and diving after insects and other small animals, which they bite with their red-tipped teeth. Water shrews have thick, velvety fur which keeps the water out.

◄ Herons sometimes eat all the goldfish in a garden pond.

Instead of chasing its prey, the heron stands perfectly still and watches. Its long legs look like sticks to the fish, voles, frogs and other small creatures that it preys on. Unafraid, they come dangerously close and the heron strikes with its sharp beak.

A heron statue keeps real herons away from the pond. ►

Although herons nest in a **colony**, they hunt on their own. So, if a heron starts eating the fish in a garden pond, the answer is to put a statue of a heron in or beside the water. Then the real heron will think that another bird is already fishing there and will go somewhere else.

THINGS TO DO IN SUMMER

Ponds are one of the most interesting places in the countryside, but even shallow ponds are dangerous, especially if you slip on mud and fall in. So be careful around ponds and never go to them alone.

Remember that you will see far more if you are quiet and patient. Exactly what you see will depend on the kind of pond you visit. The more plants there are, the better your chances of seeing some of the animals in this book. Probably the first ones you will spot are whirligig beetles which move about on the surface. If you watch them carefully, sooner or later one of them will catch something – perhaps a fly that has fallen into the water.

If a dragonfly lands near you, take a good look at it. Notice its huge eyes which will certainly be watching you! It needs extremely good eyesight to spot prey when flying at over 90 km an hour. Perhaps you will see two dragonflies joined together. This is when a male and female are mating. Damselflies are easier to see. Though brightly coloured, they have thinner bodies and fly more slowly, folding their wings back when resting (true dragonflies always keep their aeroplane shape).

Damselflies fold back their wings when resting.

The golden leaves of autumn are reflected in the pond.

Life in the pond changes dramatically in the autumn. The surrounding trees drop their leaves into the water and most of the pond plants begin to die. Many creatures burrow into the mud at the bottom of the pond to keep warm.

Some aquatic plants have seeds which float on the surface and drift away to a different part of the pond. Others have very small seeds that stick to muddy feet. The seeds may travel a long way before they fall off, especially if they are picked up by birds.

Over the years, the remains of dead plants form layers on the bottom of the pond. Unless the pond is cleaned out, it will slowly turn into a **marsh** and eventually become overgrown.

THINGS TO DO IN AUTUMN

Late autumn is a good time to examine the underworld of a pond, as a number of creatures bury themselves in the mud when the weather turns cold. Using a strong fishing net or an old soup ladle, gently scoop up some mud from the bottom of the pond and tip it into a wide container (such as a plastic ice-cream box). Among the mud, stones and decaying leaves, you will find an assortment of strange animals: hibernating whirligig and diving beetles, snails, insect larvae and various pond worms. When you have finished looking at them, put everything carefully back into the pond.

Water plants are different in many ways from other plants. Those that grow right in the pond rely on the water to hold them up. When removed from the water, they are floppy and break easily. Their leaves are thin and very delicate. Have a look among the pond plants for their seeds. Those of the water lily have air trapped inside them so that they float. The brown seeds of the yellow iris develop inside large green pods, which split into three when ripe. They have a water-repellent surface which gives them a chance to float away to a new place before they get wet and germinate.

Yellow iris seeds fall into the pond when they are ripe.

On a cold winter day there may be few signs of life in the pond.

You may see a heron stalking through the rushes or a few small wetland birds looking for reed seeds. If you are very lucky, you may catch sight of a water vole. There are not many leaves to eat in winter, so they feed mainly on roots and seeds. The water shrew remains active too. It noses about on the bottom of the pond for hibernating insects and larvae, even when the surface is frozen. And if you go along to the pond in the afternoon as the light is fading, an owl may swoop across the pond looking for water shrews and voles.

THINGS TO DO IN WINTER

If you have your own pond, it will need cleaning out at the end of the winter. Some of the plants will have grown too large and the water may be full of dead leaves. Scoop all the water out into buckets without stirring up the mud too much. Take the plants out of their pots and divide each one into two, then replant half of them in pots or baskets of fresh soil. The rest can be potted and given away. Then remove any dead leaves from the bottom and replace the plants and water, topping up the level with fresh water if necessary. While you are cleaning out the pond, be very careful not to throw away or damage any living things.

In the wild, ponds are usually too large to freeze completely. Even if the surface is covered with ice, the lower levels of water and mud remain unfrozen. However, small garden and container ponds may freeze solid, killing the wildlife in them. To stop your pond from freezing, float a block of polystyrene on the surface. Tie a weight (such as a stone) to it with a piece of string so that it does not blow away in high winds.

Dead leaves sink to the bottom and rot slowly.

Spring

Summer

Autumn

Winter

GLOSSARY

Algae Plants that have no proper stems, roots or leaves and grow in water or damp places.

Amphibians Animals that can live on land but must breed in water (for example, frogs, toads and newts).

Aquatic Living in water.

Breed To produce young.

Carnivorous Flesh eating.

Colony A group of the same kinds of animals living together.

Community A group of plants and animals that live in the same area and depend on each other.

Evaporates Dries up.

Food chain A group of living things, each of which feeds on another in the group and in turn is eaten by others.

Hibernation Spending the winter in a sleep-like state.

Larvae The young of certain animals after they have hatched from eggs but before they turn into adults (for example, tadpoles).

Mammals Animals that are warm-blooded and feed their young on milk.

Marsh Land that is always wet and that is sometimes flooded.

Mate The pairing of a male and female in order to have young.

Nectar A sweet liquid produced by flowers to attract insects.

Oxygen A gas which is present in the air and needed by all living things.

Peat A kind of soil that is made from decayed plants and is found in boggy areas.

Pollen A powder produced by the male parts of a flower, which makes the female parts develop seeds.

Pollination When the female parts of a flower receive pollen from the male parts.

Polluted Filled with poisonous or harmful substances.

Prey To hunt.

Spores Tiny seed-like grains which eventually grow into new plants.

BOOKS TO READ

Discovering Dragonflies and Damselflies by Linda Losito (Wayland, 1987).

Discovering Pond Life by Colin Hawkins (Wayland, 1989).

Frogs and Toads by Anne Smith (Wayland, 1989).

In the Pond by Sarah McKenzie (Wayland, 1985).

Life in Ponds by Althea (Dinosaur Publications, 1984).

Life in Ponds and Streams by Oliver Aston (Macdonald, 1981).

The Life Cycle of a Frog by John Williams (Wayland, 1987).

The Life Cycle of a Stickleback by Philip Parker (Wayland, 1988).

The Nature Trail Book of Ponds and Streams by Su Swallow (Usborne, 1980).

The Observer's Book of Pond Life by John Clegg (Frederick Warne, 1980).

Ponds and Streams by Judith Court (Franklin Watts, 1985).

Picture acknowledgements

All photographs were taken by Deni Bown with the exception of the following: Chris Fairclough Colour Library 6 (top), 11 (below), 19, 21 (top), 22 (top), 26; Oxford Scientific Films 6 (below), 12 (both), 16, 17 (both), 18, 20, 21 (below), 27; A.E. Wills 4, 11 (top).

INDEX